Insipid Dream

How vague
Is the thought of heaven
Becoming an insipid dream
Fading within the first breath
Oxygenating the potency

Of life's substance
Within a baby's mind

Before perspective
Could squint through the blinds
To witness blurred visions
Festering around how
A soul could be captured
Under the stamp
Of life's first impression

.

My Soul's Life

Nine months of incubation
Purified the fluids
Fountaining my youth

I wonder
How much history
My soul washed away
In the nectar sealing my presence
Inside a womb being prepped for labor

I wonder if God knew
How I'd decide to rupture
The fragile tendons knotting the thickness

Of wool woven sheets
Draping the ignorance
Of a curious mind
Questing to discover the source of an itch
By exploring how deep
A nail must dig into a scratch
Before satisfying the urge
Initiating the enviable chill of deep thought.
What could be the purpose
Of having dreams so strong

You die along with them
When you wake up

DREAM

Sentenced to life
By judgments

Exerted through force
Exhausting a heavy heart
Caged inside lovely bones
Filling out her gown

Constricting paths

Through a warping wormhole
Twirling me against contractions
Before I landed in the bed they made for me,

Dizzy spells
Influenced the slurred drip
Fountaining the drool
Eluding the grip of taste buds
Staggering my speech
As it stuttered off
The illiterate ladle my tongue formed
As I spoon fed my broken language
Against the seasoned atmosphere

Before getting sifted through

The moist palms
Of society's melting pot

.

Black Shepherd

God must've
Used an ancient thread
To knit my mind
Into complex knots
Stiff enough to
Suffocate my understanding
Of the dark toxins
Infesting my pigment

Softening thick skin
Through punctured pores
Overdosing on melanin
As black strands
Became the wool
Symbolizing my destiny
As the black Shepherd
Herding crowds of sheep
Able to hurdle the moon
Like shooting stars

Before dying
From the dreams

Wished upon them
As they free fall
Into gravitational pulls
Inside the dimensions of my imagination

.

Reminiscent

I Remember
Never being too young
To thumb through false facades
Clouding the pages
Of my mental notebook

Fingerprints stamping
The cusp of sheets I pinched
To gather my thoughts
Before fanning my visions
Into motion pictures,
For pupils to study the dialect
Invested in the illusions
My curiosity articulated
Through the depths of me

I remember being like this
For as long as I can remember
Getting tangled in trances

From bedtime instrumentals
Dancing off spinning shrines
Hovering over the wooden nest
Nurturing the forbidden fruit

That will dangle from the new leaf
Developing in the loins
Of my family tree

Even though every generation falls

A little farther from its roots
Losing touch with my heritage
To gain the traits of a model citizen

I miss the hums
Of cradled nursing times
Rocking me to sleep
Wondering
If I died in a dream
Does that become my heaven
Or will I live long enough
To sin and live amongst the demons
Building the pyramids
Within the blocks of my city
So he who sits at the top

Can be high enough to overlook us

.

PURPOSE

Waking up
In the rubbish of derailed

Trains of thought
Attempting to traffic ideas
Across an indecisive conscious
Struggling to maintain its momentum
Against uncertainties' stronghold

So its not my feet
But the track in my mind
That has blisters,

Cargo cars sync lines
That segregate the parallel tracks
Lining the blue printed voyage
To my lips
Through the source of my infatuations
Expanding the distance of thought

Using lumps of coal
From past mistakes
To fuel my will of fire into cycles,
Chugging this locomotive
Down streams of consciousness
Blowing clouded fixtures
Big enough to frame life
And what it truly means ,
But how tight

Was the grip
Of iron hands locked
Between the knuckles of rotting couplings
Tugging these
Bottled emotions along corroded rail lines
Hoping shifting cars never rock off track
And ideas go a stray
Or rattle the glass enough to break
Before my lips

Could deliver the message

.

SILENT

Silent endeavors
Quenched smiles
To grin and bear
My failure to understand
How frail tissue
Couldn't decompose the sodium
In tormented tears
Dripped off the cheek
Of an unbegotten soul
Sentenced to war with himself
Until he masters how to tame
A spontaneous mind

What is the purpose
Of lessons learned
But not remembered?
Or strands of knowledge
Becoming the opposing force
To a body already set in motion?

How far would you go to save yourself
Cleansing your being
In rich soil
After diving head first
Into murky water

WINDOW COMPLEX

I had a tinted-window complex
Watching life through distorted lenses
Cradling perceptions
In a canister of ignorance
Outlining the glass box frames
Casing my perspective

Trying to capture
Happiness
And harvest it in a jar
Like lighting bugs
Picnicking on an open field

Held down by summer nights
But some things
Were just meant to be free
.

MAYBE

Maybe it was that house
Planted firmly
On 65th and 18th street,
Maybe it was
How big my room was,
Or how those walls
Held hands to quarantine my obsession
With living on my knees
As my imagination buffered visions
That possessed my loneliness
Inside a fixated desire for space

Maybe I was a little too quiet
Playing with train sets
Taking Thomas off the track
"Cuz" the wooden floor
Made the clunking sound I wanted
Rolling over grooves

Paneling wooden floors
Picking up power rangers
To protect them from little green soldiers
Patrolling the streets
With Woody and Buzz Lightyear

Looking for Lance Armstrong
Around Hotwheels tracks
Where remote control cars
Raced until they flew off course
Landing in Lego towns
Filled with Tonka trucks
Dumping building blocks for Lego men
Sitting on the roof of toy chests
Watching the evening drive-in movie
Staring at the silhouettes
Of everything in motion
As the sun peeked through my window
.

NAIVE

I was naive
To my mother's attempt to
Protect my purity,
As if she didn't hear
The monsters outside my window
Creating the theme music
To a long night of suspense
Seeping through window seals
As keys jingled and swayed
Alongside nervous energy

Initiated conversations
Set the tone
Before the bass dropped
As tussles added percussion
To the late-night instrumentals
From muffled aggravation
Clashing trash cans
While the audience spectated
Through the dark slits
Of inconspicuous blinds
That suddenly seemed to have
Lost their light

I remember
How she tried to drown it out
With loud noises
Watching Martin
Or listening to Luther
So King Jr
Could have a dream

.

SPEECHLESS

Lost in the illusion of
How the grip of her eyes
Pinched knots in my throat
Stifling the stroke of deep breaths
No longer able to rub the fine hairs
Harmonizing my vocal box

Tangling my wit
Inside the warmth of moments
Chilled through subtle inhales
Sucked between arched lips
Preparing to save me
With an ice breaking rebuttal
Aiming to unshackle cold feet

But ambitions
Were trapped inside drifting clouds
Stranded upstream,
Wondering how her words felt
Swimming over taste buds
Underlying the river of thought
Stroking her tongue
Producing beautiful instrumentals

Harmonizing silent whispers of sweet nothings
Echoing against speechless moments
Fogging the glass of a transparent face

.

THROUGH MY MIND

Polished cuticles
Fumigated aromas
Off illuminated steps
Strong enough to

Peel a vivid depiction
Off its cloudy canvas
Women are queens
Because they control the minds
Of those that keep them in theirs
Surrendering sight
As I tugged on eyelash strings
Thickening blinds
Attempting to seal cracked windows
From vented toxins
Stuck in eye sockets
Hoarding timid thoughts
Behind pupils that dilate
Every time the sun shines
Through the sparkle in her eyes
Stashing moments
Smeared in father time's watch
Saving face in safety deposit boxes
Locked in the basement
Of my memory bank

Praying the happiness.
That flew around my mind
Never would set itself free

.

YOUNG IDEAS

I mean
How could you
Hold something all night
And wake up alone

Funny how
Long walks in the park
Holding hands
Double coned ice-cream swirls
Was my idea of happily ever after

Funny how
I was so helpless
Yet I never felt I needed it
I couldn't see
That my actions were
Desperate pleas to my sanity

And that ,
Lost souls would forever damage me

Funny how
I lost my smile
The more I grew
I treated women like
They were doing me a favor

Nobody ever listened
I just needed a few minutes
Don't push me away

My heart is
Already paw printed
My sheets are already
Soaked from tears
I drowned in
My dreams seemed augmented
Yet still something I could never fit in

Funny how
I thought of her so much
If she didn't act how I imagined
I'd assume she wasn't being herself

Funny how
Emotions are flows of energy
And how we form
Dams with our lies
Suffocating our spirit
Then wonder how we've become
Shy and timid

ART

Eyes drool over
Sharp depictions
Plugging worm holes
Saturated in the flavors
Defining her contrast
As I
Got lost in pigments
Sun glares
Created off the soft tone
Of her brown skin

She's my,
Poetry in motion
The closed book
I shouldn't judge by the cover
Provoking my curiosity
To fill in blanks perfecting the picture
Hanging in my frame of mind

Struggling to fathom
How her hips sway
Into the wind
Carrying those thick curls
As if

The breeze
Was twirling them
Around its' finger
As my eyes
Follow the trance
While trying to climb
The whining staircase

Hoping to find,
Beauty in her mind
Cuz her body is just a shell
Meant to be cracked and explored

But her mind
Is a twisted fixation of desire
Feeding off the weakness
Inside the shell
Of a man's ego
Forcing you to grow
Through your flaws
To become worthy of her love.
But without that mind,
Her body will forever be
Something that looks nice hung on a wall

.

WISHFUL THINKING
Seems like
Staring into frames
Only marginalized my perception.
How could I get a feel for the art
When my hand never touched the canvas?

I never watched
My grasp sink into love handles
Holding me in place
While arching fingers
Until they hook and lock

Digging into her pelvic tissue
Anchoring my position of power
Trying to wring her fluids out
Twisting swaying hips
To stir up emotion
As it drips from the fountain

I never thought of
The sins I'd commit to taste the forbidden fruit
How the cherry blossoms would bloom
Over the casket of my innocence
From giving pieces of myself

To promises of never being alone.
But the devil is a liar
And I hope
I didn't just sell him my soul

.

NUTRITION

I wonder how nerves
Tasted on her tongue
As deep breathes
Pushed fear
Over the hill of full lips
Separating every word
She uttered
Sealing messages
Between the lines
Of small talk

Pitching under tones
Over the striking point
Of judgement's index finger
But my hands
Will only frame your figure

Humming as I
Explored her temple
Encouraging her to listen to feelings
Sliding down the side of her neck
Biting at tissue trailing shoulders
On my way to the puppet show
From high beams
Mounted to lamp posts

As I strolled through the park
Leaving chills
Down the path I created
As wind tickled chilled water
Dripping behind
Land marks scattered
From the staggered steps
Of a wandering tongue
Approaching the crease of hills
That rise during sunsets,

Rising from the foot
Hoping not to lose balance
Pacing strides to the well

Closed eyes
Leaned over lips
kissing granted wishes
Sampling strokes of genius
After taste buds ingested,
Fountains of her youth

Dreaming of love
I always wanted to please
I never wanted

What chose to loved me back
To ever have a reason to leave

.

LOVES' DECEIT

I still sleep in fetal position
Cloaked inside the womb
Of warm sheets
Trying to induce a coma
Deep enough to numb the feeling
Of how voices rub the wooden plank
Under my door
As pacing shadows
Conquer the light
Flickering in distress
While screaming floorboards
Squeal beneath advancing footsteps
Tilting them in and out of place
Persuading the rocking motion
Not able to cradle me
To sleep

Hunting for inner peace
Through interchangeable pieces
That prophesize the puzzling factors
Allowing an open mind to comfort me
Through the tremors of verbal onslaughts
Denying the silence I need

To rest in peace
Instead I had to sit through
My ideas of love

Falling to pieces
Wondering why the glowing box I idolized
Never shed light
On this form of affection
Love was always warm and sweet
Television never shared this image

I never witnessed
How bitter
A cool breeze cliff diving
Off pride's cold shoulder
Could level a house
With makeshift avalanches
Real enough to traumatize

A fickle dream

LOVE TO ME

I've always struggled
Putting real life
Against the equation of thought
Or maybe
I spent too much time in my head

Staring into the framework
Of moving pictures
What exactly is love to me?
My philosophies couldn't take rejection

I never handled a broken heart
But mine has had a couple bruises
That still gives me a little pain
So I shy away from expressing emotion
In fear of a Texas holdup
How many steps are left
Before we'd have to
Draw conclusions
Dancing around awkward moments
Not yet realizing
That women aren't queens
Just diamonds in a rough hand

Men aren't kings
Just jacks of many trades
To the bartering system
Of their own development
Trying to find balance
Between knowledge and emotion
Only caused friction within me

.

DEMONS

I hate that demons still live here
Rubbing my back like
It's okay to give what you take in
Better yet
It's even better
To remove the knives
Stiffening your spine
As you smile
To dignify the strength
You refuse to admit
Is also your weakness

I hate that they sit here
Whispering me into lectures
From thin air
Clouding my atmosphere
As I use the smoke to
Daydream through nightmares
Bench pressing deep breaths
Until my lips locked
Securing wishes
That tend to drift
Toward dark skies

I wish they left me in this
Created space
The exit route

I carved deep inside my head
Maybe then
Public places wouldn't haunt me
Maybe I could blend in with flavors
I was once too bitter to taste
Realizing how
Things that may not seem alike
Could still mix in the belly of laughter

Cause all I ever wanted
Was to be accepted
But not for being alike
But more so recognized
For being infected with the real
Emulating my genuine nature

I'm tired of sitting in sweet nothings
Rotting mental cavities
Trying to heal wounds
With forgiving thoughts
That leave me aching
As I try to rest pain in peace

When I should've of inflicted pain
To rest peacefully

Loneliness antagonized my genius
Living with this fear of speaking
Feeling like
I'm harboring the curse of dreaming
Labeled a weirdo
For placing my mind over
What coolness felt mattered
They'll never feel me
Through the baptism
In society's sin
As I struggle to maintain

My faith in self
Yet, those same demonic voices
Would still convince me to change

.

FRUSTRATION

But
I mastered the art of
Suppressing demons
Inside visions so vivid
You could see the frayed strands
Spiking the rope
Webbing my dreamcatcher

This

Idealistic fixture
Dangled from the ceiling of my mind
Like a chandelier flickering

Through surges of light
Exposing the visual working of my nerves
Triggering seizures
As I failed to control my actions
Living with the fear of biting my tongue

Watching full rolls of film
Unravel suspenseful plots
Before my eyes cut the footage
Breaking the connection
My attention was glued to

But
The revolution won't be televised
Hard to unmask a man
Willing to massacre his characteristics
To conform to the methods
Of the like-minded

.

PRIDE

This is the art
Of unmasking thoughts
That lashed out
Behind eyelids that snapped
Like cameras to capture
How eyes are able to devour
Moments inside glass prisms
Magnifying glimmers of sunlight
Through dilated episodes
Unraveling the bandages
Concealing historic wounds
Ruptured by the friction of motion

I remember
Holding my blinds up
To cancel the risk
Of blinks
Ruining my disguise

I needed to portray strength
Against the things that hurt me
I refused to allow the weight
Of what I held in
Crush the levy

Damming tear ducts
Against the might of tidal waves
Behind the tone of thunderstorms
Trying to stream weakness down my face

Crying my way to bus stops
Letting tears
Wash the perfume
Off the stretched collar
Of shirts I tucked under my hoodie
From morning hugs
That never loved me
Silence hid the frantic pitch in my voice
Bowed head hid puffy eyes
Sipping tears
Hoping drunk bodies
Speak sober minds
As I take shots of anger
That burned so bad going down
It loosened the things
I had to get off my chest

To what measure must a man
Defend his wife
To what measure
Should a woman
Justify her man
How could I not feel envy
When favoritism
Poisoned the remedy
Fueling toxins
That overheated my soul

.

HUNG JURY

If I promise to tell the truth
The whole truth
Nothing but the truth
Would you help me God ?

Help me take a stand
As I approach it
With knots in my throat
From truths too hard to swallow
Trying to regurgitate what I can
As questions nailed me to events
Where paths may have been crossed

Like where my mind went
After my parents told me
They couldn't afford my idea
Of acceptance
And two-cent suggestions
Weren't enough to buy friendships
Pleading my case
To my better judgment
Proceedings went to the higher court
As I relied on a jury of my peers
Struggling to maintain my posture

When nerves began to fidget
And eyes wander,
To avoid dripping liquid
To cool down an overworked spirit
Battling resentment

Funny how
A man's path through life
Is forged by
How he chose to be wrong
But what shakes the strings
That transfer a limp puppet into motion?

I wonder if the devil's nectar
Is as rich as the emotions we idolize
We act as if it's natural
To dissociate ourselves
From our own sinister plots

But
If I admit to weak moments
And embrace the wrath
That will fall upon me
And stand strong in honor
Of what I once believed
Would they find me guilty?

If I confess
My pride was stronger
Than hanging my head
Over the banister
Looking for sympathy
From people who don't know me
Or the slightest bit how I feel

Living in a world
God didn't build me for
Fighting for justification
Leaves me sore
I cry alone in the dark
When the pain won't allow me to sleep
If I turn and face the people
Whose opinions hold my life
With tears in my eyes
And my heart in my mouth
And ask a simple question

If the only way into heaven
Was remembering who you were
Before life extorted your kindness,
Would your answer be able set you free?

If the room fell deaf
Would that indicate a hung jury?

PENMANSHIP

Dipping angel feathered stems
Into bottled emotions
Helped me build
Better relationships with myself

Channeling the courage
To put my life on display
Just to watch people analyze my efforts
Through the rim of
Thick Coke bottle lenses
That only seemed to
Magnify imperfections against the glass
Framing my visions

But how can you critique me
If I'm a work of art
If God gave me life
And left it up to me to make it beautiful
After a mind refuses to casket
The scented aromas of deceased thoughts
Trapped in a repetitious cycle of treason
Every time I chose not to speak
Sheltering my insecurities

Inside the company I invited in
Never noticing how much
Of your mind is the gullible factor
That fails to get equated
When life forces you
To show your work
Under problems that over estimate you

.

SHELL

Oh how I struggled
To maintain my posture
During the pokes
Of index fingers
Defining my lack of balance
Against the wall I bled out on
Feeling like humpty dumpty
As he fell past
A stone layered wall
Before hitting the sticks
That broke his bones
Trying to use words
To sweet talk the pain
Out of hurting me

My emotions became the yolk
Leaking out of crumbled egg shells
Nesting in stuffed trashcans

Cuz,
The black ink I casted
Couldn't conquer the light
Within vivid notions
Twisting the façade of life
As the stars aligned in my head
Gaseous compounds
Created the perception
Of the lucrative thoughts
Collapsing onto
Loose sheets of paper
Fusing chaotic renditions
With a stable mind

.

YEARN

I just wanted affection
I needed more
Than any woman could ever give me
I never learned how it felt
When a woman truly cared
My resentment never allowed
My mother to show me

Drowning my depression
In lead poison
Dripped the meaning of life
Into the open wounds
My past neglected
Venting my aggression
Through the slits of lined paper
Bleeding toxins out of a cluttered mind
Smothering wisdom
Inside a crowded train of thought
In fear of missing its stop.

Like my heart
The first time she responded,
Staring at the message,
As tingles
Coarse through the tips of fingers
As they knock against the keys
Listening for the clicks
To the right combination,
I knew how important it was to listen

Make her feel comfortable
To expose what life made her
I knew I had to let her show me
Who she didn't want to be anymore

My first relationship
Was tangled in the web
I was the dreamcatcher
Filtering her nightmares
From the strands of herself
I was stuck in,
Trying to fight my way free
As she whispered
" preserve your energy"
Shedding tears

Trying to loosen the bondage
Made the cuts deeper
It was too late to save my heart
From being gently placed
Into the hands of its murderer

.

LOVE'S INFRACTION

Can I call it love
When I feel
If you were ever to leave
I'd force my soul
To bury emotion
Under all of the tissue in my chest
To suppress the pain
Of a broken heart
Drowning inside of its own sorrow
While silent tears caught in the fibers,

Scream for help
Clogging slow leaks
So emotions don't seep
Through the ribs caging them,

Until I gather six blessings
Strong enough to carry
The wreckage of a capsized relationship
Away from a guilty conscious
Dropping red roses weeping violet tears
That drag memories down the cheek
Of blushing petals
Just before they crumble

Under the pressure of defeat
To constitute a diminished love

But they say to look back at life
And to smile is to live twice
So to experience feelings of freedom
Counting loose steps
Down rocky roads
As we stumbled over crushed petals
Dropped from nature's romantic gesture
To honor a match made in heaven
Allowing a young man
To get lost inside the bond of held hands
Even when I found myself
Getting lost in an infatuation,

My eyes would travel
Across the distinctive way her body curved
From its hidden language ,
Like how my fingers
Would depict my native tongue
On the lines of fallen trees
Replenishing the oxygen
My words always seemed to take away

Instigating the pleasures
Of a young love trapped in the thought
And what's more vivid than a kid's vision

Running through palaces
With a queen's princess
The premature expectation of a woman
Before reality settles the dust
You organized your thoughts in

IDOLIZE

Is it not wise
To idolize perfection?
Is it not wise
To want to be happy?
Can you find someone
Able to create what it means to you ?
Will you be humble enough to accept it?

My rush to feel
What's owed to me
Allowed words
To get twisted inside the swirl
Of pockets of wind
That escape puckered lips
Kissing departing courtships
Transporting my hopes for us
Across oceans of pavement
Only to
Deliver mixed emotions

Is it not wise to seek the truth?
Am I wrong for wanting you
To conduct the driving force
Behind my happiness?

Are you that tainted
That you don't think
This effort could be for you
I wonder if
The beauty of a mockingbird
Relies on its role model
Was the mockery made of me
A reflection of what I was
Or what she thought of me?

.

PINS AND NEEDLES

Cupid's arrow
Was the first form of lethal injection

Twisting tornados
Around the bark of wooden shafts
Against spiraling points
Piercing through reality
Creating winds capable of
Sweeping a dream off its feet

After needles
Puncture flesh
Injecting marinated serums
Of eye candy

Around the tip
Crafting mans demise
Off the whim of assumption
Becoming the canvas
Images copy and paste themselves onto
Manifesting a repetitious cycle of thought
Idealizing the process of affection

But, Moments you remain stuck in
Only manage to teach you
How to love them

Cupids arrow was the first form of lethal injection
Because it leaves you absent-minded

I know my issues with love
Was the yearn for someone
To justify what I already thought of myself

I'd get so stuck in daydreams
Of how I thought things would go
Only to wake up with pins and needles
That made me think my nightmares
Were the sweetest of dreams

.

AIR

How can words
Sit on air too thin
To carry meaning

How deep are breaths
Whisking away
The potency of my soul's verbal art
Portraying emotions
Tangled within the bristles
Arching my tongue
Splashing images of my heart
Against the window pane
Framing a window of opportunity
Set in stones layering her fortress

My essence whistled between cracks
Echoing silent alarms
Filling a vacant temple
Struggling to preserve the scent
Of intrusion.

I wanted her
To open those doors for me
Crafting my will through spoken word
Flooding her mind
With poetic renditions
Until her eyes water up with content
Providing me with the reaction I now
Love to feel
But
She only reached for doses of me
To numb her inflictions,

Sips of my remedy
Refilled her self-esteem
Keeping me in rotation
The abused became the abuser
Looping my role inside a vicious cycle
Even my attempts to back pedal
Only recycled my position
In the hand I was dealt,

Extorting my kindness
To balance out emotional debts
Harboring the fugitive
That destroyed her palace
And
No matter how I tried to forgive
No matter how much I felt
My love was stronger than his
We were just kids playing with fire
Not realizing our mistakes will burn
For eternity

.

BROKEN

Watching soot
Crumble off the burning stake
Spite shoved through my heart
Dying inside phases of distortion

Life's lonely breeze
Swept how I felt aside
because I still missed her
How weak was I,
I never kissed her

Addicted to the idea
Of how a woman's elixir
Could heal my soul,

Only to find
It was the only drug
Able to abandon me
While I was still high

.

INFLICTION

Documenting jolts
Jumping off the Richterscale
Scribbling my life on graphing paper
Trying to triangulate
The last time love felt real

Before she acted like
We never happened,
And I'd accuse her
Of being like everyone else

Reaching for a straw
Able to siphon the emotions
I had poured at her feet
Back through the trunk
Drowning the elephant in the room,
As I shouldered
The weight of my world
As it fell
Out of orbit

.

CONFUSION

Curiosity
Loosened fear's grip
Around lures dragging my mind
Through evacuated spaces
Engulfing misery's dense
Gravitational pulls
Against tranquil postures
Paralyzing progression
Inside the box framed perspectives
I couldn't seem to escape.

Sheltering my pain
In the belief
That people were meant to hurt me,
Forcing cries for help
To spill from the top of toy chests
Through silent sniffles
Waiting for someone to care enough
To come check on me
And see the cracked window
I planted to stir confusion
I needed to hear
Love's frantic pitch searching
For reality to defy assumption

I wanted the world
To work how I envisioned it
I thought my thinking was simple enough
After all who would grant me
The ability to comprehend
How the purpose of seeking the light
Is to eventually become it

.

COOL

Growing to idolize
How cool emulated
Off the persona
Housing clever words
That slid down slippery lanes
Could laminate a wet tongue

Striking pin-up girls
Off the twisted fate
Leaving marks
On the spot
As she

Begun to fall through gazes
Staring past literation
As she daydreamed about dates

I wanted that kind of effect
On people
But who did I follow?
When my conscious
Didn't allow me
To think for myself,
When television
Tunneled my vision
Into thinking nothing else

When glasses suggested
I needed a little more help
Staring through coke bottle frames
That allowed people to
Count the freckles on my face
From lenses that
Hang over the banister
Of a greasy nose
Overseeing a crooked smile
Hiding inside the chubby cheeks
Of a chunky kid
Looking to hide behind

A timid smile,

And an image
He created to protect feelings
Too weak to defend themselves

.

PEER PRESSURE

Life's pressure peered
Through thoughts of grandeur
Soaking my presence inside
Dimensional gaps
Dominating empty spaces,

Revamping remedies
Diluting murky elixirs
Trying to level
Chemical imbalances
Offsetting my strides
Toward performing rituals
Dignifying the properties
Of a man

.

MATURING

How deep
Must I dig
After cracking the shell
Hugging a closed mind
Before obtaining
Grooves deep enough
To carve lifelines
Into the soul of dead trees
Isolating distress codes
Inside artistic lectures
Exposing the effects
Of conflictual tales
Chastising repetitious cycles
Of how chasing my tail
Never allowed me to find myself,

Lucid visions
Peer through prisms
Stacking layers of cataract
Obstructing points of view
Between foresight
And the darkness within me,

Clouded mind
Prepping brain storms
Big enough to fill voids
With justifications
Sheltering sins committed
Onto thyself,
Becoming too cool
For daydreams playing hero
With the woman I crushed on
Or the Kung Fu fights

Between number 2 pencils
During class
Wondering when
My superpowers would surface
So I could gracefully take down bullies
All the while ignoring the one

I've become

.

DREAMER

What if
Life was just a dream
And when you fell asleep
You actually woke up
Making the sin in not dreaming
The possibility of eternal darkness
Becoming your hell

But what happens to the dreamer
Pouring his aura into life's pitcher
To see if
At the half way point
It felt half empty

How could something
So simple contain me
This is nothing more then an instrument
Used to obstruct my vision
Once I moved it out my way
I became free from my prism

Society won't wear my pain
To cosign fashion statements
Signifying my talent as the diamond
They saw through the rough tone
Of dirty skin
But my efforts
To work hard

To be more like them
In turn cleaning me up
To shine on the finger
Of the hand
That was able to pull me up
Just to sit me back in a box
After my trend is up

It's amazing
How much
They are able to control what you see
And the patterns in which
You're trained to think
But what they can't control
Is perception
Life is personal
Because we all

Digest it a little differently

My mind is the
Fixated infringement
Set to bend the laws
That support society's structure
I was born a Martian
In a marginalized margin
Where I took my pen
And lead my emotions
To conclude organized notes
Could harmonize life's instrumental

What if
Your afterlife
Was the collage of memories
You've saved while living
Subjecting yourself to eternal
Happiness or torment
Would you still fear death ?

.

ANOINTED

Chest knocking between my knees
As we walked down to my house
What does she expect from me
Will it be like
It is on TV?
Should I play music
And lick her softly
As I caress her skin

We're at my door now
I'm contemplating
A reconsider
Hands fiddling keys
Hoping I'm big enough
Hoping she assumes a position
Similar to the videos I've studied
So I could attempt to implement my dominance
Catch the rhythm to her song
And let her sing along

Walking into my room
She sits on my twin mattress
On the wooden frame
I had since
I used to wash it in my sleep
And wake up forgetting to dry it
As she asks if I'm nervous
Relieved as I agree
She starts to undress
And say it's okay

Watching her
Disappear beneath the sheets
I stripped to my boxers,
Trying to hide my discomfort
But she wanted to see

Staring at her serious face
I dropped my boxers,
She smiles pulling back the sheets
No music as I climb in
No movie scenes
Just a broke stroke
Trying to maintain its dignity

But couldn't last long
Short lived victories upset me

I felt no different
Thought it would make me a man,
My first time wasn't magical
But worth every second

I became a man
When I stopped defining it with accomplishments
And started accommodating the mindset
.

STALEMATES

Stalemates triggered my urge
To fidget with ideals

The physical act of
Climbing into my thoughts
Hoping to sit with
The happiness I created
While playing God
in my realm of creativity

But how vivid is my perspective
Walking through life
Hoping what I see
Is what I made it

Should I have been a realist
Submitting to pain
Becoming another stain
Drying up on a curb
As another one of
God's spitting images
For the media to
Hose me down with propaganda

And bleach me with diluted theories
For opposing the power that
Suppresses me

The American dream
Was created in the smoke
That settled the war over
Who will control this land
Governed by the fear of inferior genetics
The very day cruelty became power
And the forbidden fruits layer of pain
began to unfurl
I hope beliefs in mustard seeds
Muster up the courage I need
To love the history
For all the dirt on both sides
Earthing the seeds
Harvesting a past we refuse to forgive
Or the innocent leaves
That fall victim to the breeze of life

.

STRANDED
I really want you to feel,
How my disassociation
Left me disoriented
My failures to build relationships
In what,
Glass bottle frames reflected
Capsized my life jacket
In pools of darkness
As I drifted through death
Daydreaming of nightmares
Caught in a loop
Returning me to my demise
After venturing through
White lights of nothingness
Traumatized by the stale scent
of the mess I made
After I
Became my own protagonist
Manifesting my fears
Inside empty spaces
The back story
To how I became my own
Worst enemy
Feeling helpless
In rooms

Full of my own creations

It must've been
The emotions of God
That shivered my body into a ball
Hoping someone
Would save me
Even though
I came out unscathed
The darkness in my skin
Will forever taint me

.

SOUTHERN WINDS

Those southern winds
Must still hum negro spirituals
Through hues that whistle
as they squeeze
Between the puckered gaps
Of tightly knit trees
Easing the aches and pains
Of limp branches
Deformed from
Old shrines that no longer dangle
at their finger tips

Society itself
Is like a forest really
those who study change
Colonized our family trees
So they know
when forbidden fruits
Are seasoned enough
To be picked alive
Initiating the destruction
Of manipulated leaves
Stained by nature
To obtain different shades

Like those
Herds of clouds
That still surf channeled breezes
Under the moonlight they shade out
Becoming the ancient sheep
Black souls counted
Before resting in peace
I bet if they could "television"
They'd expose how its on repeat
The reason the revolution
Won't be televised
Because your mind is unable
To expand any further
Than the images framed
Inside the box your focus is trapped in

Getting you to stare at technology
Is how they mastered the reaping
Of the benefit behind.
inserting their idea of life
Inside the heart of distraction
Molding clouded minds
To portray Illustrations
For inquisitive retinas
To digest visions for a mind to perceive

Only this Rorschach test
Teaches you how to think

But I refuse
To have my roots severed
My family tree
has already been struck
By lightning
Dividing me from one of my seeds
Pain hurts cuz it can't kill you
The same way knowledge can't heal you
Just prolongs the issue
Because eventually you'll still die
My idea of peace
Escapes me sometimes
I sum up my thoughts
To seal the rants sometimes
I lose hope
In the strength of my fingertips
I don't reach to grab dreams
As they fade sometimes
I no longer wake in a panic
My dreams don't have the power
To kill me before I wake
Leaving me damaged before sunrise

I realized that I am defeated
If I continued to hang my head
And blame everything on the fact
I ain't like them
Then the lynching will continue to repeat

Earth will not be my purgatory

I vow to love humanity
With the respect I have for me
If I Die for that
Then make sure they say I died
With my head up straight
Ten toes deep
With the biggest smile

.

MOON

I'm a warrior
Of the moon
Doused in ancient cloaks
Nullifying the powers of the sun
Battling things that hide in the shade
Masking what you had to become;

A black child's
Nappy headed cerebral
Intertwined universal hues
Raining shooting stars
Vivid enough to
Meditate with
Manifested auras
Of distant dreams

But poverty
Dampens the free will
Of his thoughts

And,
Lack of parenting
Would loosen

His grip on optimism
Silver spoons

Only fed emptiness
As food for thought
Inside privileged urban households

Conform,
Or be reformed
What kind of freedom
Reaps a caged bird
Never anointed by life
For overcoming the bar exam
Surpassing the cage
to remain under the judgment of God

Or his creations
Observing chess moves
From a checkered hand

BLACK YOUTH

What's the geography
Sculpting the landscape
Of hills and valleys

Callousing hands
Gripping the street
Performing reps
Pushing the weight of the world
Off my back
Over working
The lacerations in my spine
Allowing my lifeline
To flex its mobility
Through the auxiliary cord
Shifting discs
Could never skip on

Splitting pavements
Between cut eyes
Dismantling my innocence
As I paddled my pity boat

Adults shielding blessings
From God's sin
Speaking to cold stares
Treating me like the plague
Building superiority complexes
To compound society's makeup
Powdering ugly features
To save face,

Crying while
Getting chastised
Through lectures
Molding margins
From parental guidance
Gauging my quest for peace and love
To dive inward
Because
They'll only see you
As a N-word

And how my
Plea for acceptance
Was weakness
I was the only thing
I needed to accept

I used to think my black
Was defective
My antics
Tugged at the hems
Of what I hoped
Still existed in people
But it would only leave me defeated

MIRRORS

Society harvests
The masking agents
Of self reflection;

What kind of surfaces
Do you exist on?
Because;
How you decide to
Respect the living
Is how you've decided to
Respect your own life
How you handle things
Is how you'll be handled
Karma is a reflection of self

Foreign steps
Pillage through life
Imprinting the crust
Of earth's ceiling
Everything you see
Is upside down
If gravity was to ever glitch
We'd fall into space

Perceptions of light shows
Perfected trick shots
Through magnifying glasses
Swallowed in the black hole
Of dilated pupils
Triangulating vast spectrums
To narrow vivid points
Twisting images through the spiral
Before pinning photos
Against the back of your mind
For reflection

What picture will you paint
When it's time to reflect on
What you are ?

.

CLOUDY VISION

I remember
Crumbling dead trees
Uprooting encrypted prophecies
Shadowing the image of crop circles
Spread across
The belly of my backwood

Twisting my fate
To get abducted
By foreign influences

After thumbnails
Dive into the roof
Of papier-mâché coffins
To crop the image
Grave-robbing Dutches
Of their guts
To stash veggies
Inside the bandages
That mummified my intention
To perform rituals
To enhance mental health

Cremating my creations
Over bonfires
Steaming my
Smoke infested deep breaths
Oxygenating the belief
In puckered lips
Being able to
Tug on gusts of wind
Strong enough to pull empty clouds
Through the forbidden forest
To shelter the dreams
My mind had no home for

Watching how
Orange roses bloomed
So vividly
When stems rested
In oral vases
Soaking the root
As my regrets
Sizzled on the
Peeling skin of petals
Ashing the weight of dust
As embers
Ride clouds of smoke

Kiting Chinese lanterns
Through ceremonies
That allowed my emotions
To drift away

I pulled life
From the blunt
Riding the high
Until it was done,
Then latching on to another host
I became what I was running from
Drowning in feelings
I became too weak to tread
With all those leeches
On my back
Anchoring my defeat

As I plummet
Through hell
Picking leeches off
As they become weak
Saving them for
The belly of the beast
Sipping the aromas
Of all the secrets in me they ate

Through flickering roses
Blooming against the wind
Paying respects to my pain

Watching the ashes drip
Is like watching
The weight fall off my back
As that rose got to my lips

I prepared to kiss death,

Burying
The worst parts of me in that Dutch
I gained a habit through that rush
And started relying on it
A little too much

I had to find something
I loved more than freedom itself

.

NEW LOVE

Spinning tires
Twisting the fabric
Of time and space
Traveling through wormholes
Glitching through patches of smoke
That captures light
After sunshine fades
Against the pavement

Exposing the twinkle
In the eyes of shooting stars
Invading my rear view
As I ran down taillights
Cluttering my atmosphere

I loved how
My eyes line danced
On the edge of sight
While hands sat steady
Behind knuckles
Dictating my direction
Through gaps
As the lost streak of light

Searching for enough darkness
To isolate its shine

How it must feel
When thread strings
Dig into the ripples of pavement,
As tires rotate the grip needed
To send a shuttle into motion
Switching gears through
Turbulent transitions of chaos,
Skipping through reality
With one hand taming the beast
While the other one riles it up
Stuffing me into my seat
Breathing balls of fire
As she peaks

These visions were somewhere
The weed couldn't take me
Or feel the voids in my pocket
Counting on change
To support my odds
But still hoping they never fall through

Because no matter how many people
Step over a penny

It never loses its value
It will always pay for the thought

WET DREAMING

Wet paint
Mocked the gazing eyes
Of spectators
Star struck by the crystals
Sprinkled throughout the coat
Of her chassis

Gliding through the city
As sunshine envies
How it reflects
Off the flared hips
Defining her curves
With thick thighs
Showing a little leg
Between the gaps of stiff suspension
Teasing fans lost in her frame
Allowing her to maneuver

Smoothly through cracked foundations
As she catwalks
Down runways
Demanding attention
From every step
That clicked through the kisses

She blessed the pavement with

Jet black eyelashes protect
The windows to her soul
Concealing me deep in her mind
I maintain her figure
I take the time to wash her up
Keep her well kept
But looks ain't everything
So I take the time
To fondle her mind
So her walk demands attention
900 horses idling
Through her windpipes
Harmonized whistles as she peaks
When I hit her spot
Exhaust crackling
As hop on and off the throttle
Hitting it just right
So she squirts fireballs
Every time I switch positions of the stick
Replanting my feet onto the mat
To maintain my position

She represents me
I must keep her happy.

I must keep her healthy.
At least that's how it was in my mind
Cars are the empty canvases
For your personality to consume
Take your time
And get it the way you want it
I've never owned such a beauty
But I've dreamed so much about it
I convinced myself
It would feel like this

Trying to build a woman
That wouldn't leave me
After I made her special
Investing my commitment
Into the potential I saw
And reaping the benefits
Of what I knew was possible
I give her what she needs
We live in peace
My heart can keep
Its remaining pieces
And maybe
Putting her together
Will become the tool that fixes me

FALLEN STAR

How long
Will descending clouds
Have to cry
Before becoming light enough
To keep dreams a float,
Staring into endless pits of thought
As the depths of reality
Start sinking in,

But still not yet able
To fathom
My comfort in moments
Framed inside a line of sight
Paralyzed by motion
Focusing the scope
On images my pupils
Weren't built to capture

What upholds
Your perception of life?
What would happen
To your beliefs
If reality opposed
What you never imagined ?

Being forced to accept
Fraying hairs
Spiking the fabric
Along the cloth your mother
Cut you from

They never told me
Following your heart
Was just as dangerous
As following the herd

.

HER PAIN

I never seen pain illustrated so vividly
Watching her voice tremble
Like the sound of his tires
Skipping the pavement

As her lips quivered
Like the grip of his hands
Shaking against the steering wheel
As she gasps before
Choking on the knot in her throat
From tangled emotions
Submitting her tongue into locks

Like the brakes he slammed on
Hoping her taste buds
Had enough traction
To make statements stick
To the asphalt
"If it wasn't for this
It wouldn't of happened .."
Echoing against silent rebuttals
Prepping her mouth to bite the bullet
Thickening saliva against her gums
As it rises to the pearly white pills

She refuses to swallow

Diluting toxins
Within the clear syrup
Self-inflicting it's potency
As she sips
From her fluctuating jar of misery
Expanding as tears
Line the crack of her mouth
Chasing the shot

Like the sound the collision
Breaking her heart
Like the steering wheel
That broke his
After the airbag missed his calling
While God made his
Killing two birds with one stone
As she dies right along with him

.

MY PLACE

I felt,
Eggshells crackle
Under shuffling feet
Tiptoeing across snake skinned tiles
Layering the dungeon
I had to carry the weight
Of an overbearing message through,

Even after her smile
Lived long enough to notice
That her happiness
Didn't follow me

Was it meant,
For me to anchor news
Channeling my destiny
To halt her
Regularly scheduled program
To broadcast fractured limbs
Crippling her family tree

Blurred resolutions
Obstructed visuals
Of the revolution

Behind my eyes
Revoking my ability to
Verbalize scenes
Looping behind lenses
Drowning in emotion,

I didn't have the heart
To break hers
So I told her,
Her son has been in an accident
And I'll take you to him

.

SCENE

I remember
The vivid contrast
Of blank stares
Contaminating suspense's
Failure to contain effects
Breaking down bundles
Of love's manifestation,

Scattered chunks of metal
Exposed a harvested dream
Cradled inside stale dust
Clouding her judgment
Within the sight
Of what she refused to believe,

I was forced,
To watch her decompose
Under the moon lit howls
Surrounding life's prey

What lies between the crevices
Of an unfolding situation
Trapped inside time lapses

When applied to the
Back pedaling footage of memory
Guiding events along the timeline
Of chain reactions
Chasing the shadow
Of a man that died behind me

.

LIT CANDLES

Scented candles
Ascend breaths of flavored speeches
That harmonize
With the whistles of the wind
The draft of those souls
No longer able to practice life
Through the bodies they once lived in
How euphoric it is
To come in peace
Yet leave so many things

In pieces

DISCOVERY

My innocence,
Resonated with ashes
Slowly birthing clouds
Through night air,

Witnessing how,
Love's definition
Couldn't fathom itself
Within the complex equation
Digesting two souls
Through events divisible
By the common denominated
Factor of self
In order to
Shed layers of fear
To end up together
As one

But forbidden patterns
Hem the silver lining
Of mystical clouds
Holding the secrets
To why
Some dreams never break through,

Stretching my third eye
Around the definitive nature
Of something so wild and boisterous
Yet so calm and filling
I must conquer this type of love
Before I leave this world with pain
As my only receipt

.

TORN

Who am I to decipher
Poetic renditions chattering
Off vibrations
Coursing through fine hairs
Stretching patterns
Across muted voice boxes,

As my spirit
Became the air
Plucking the cords
While free falling through lines
I vowed to never cross
Verbalizing my fear of trust

Sung songs
Of hyperextended reaches
Controlling the sleeve
You wore your heart on
Breaking your falls
In and out of affectionate teases
As it suffered through beatings
Forcing your mind
To send signals of pain

To the only thing
Able to love you

So tell me,
What ricochets off the chess board
When black thoughts
Invade white clouds
Wrestling for position
Twisting tornados
That break wind
Scenting my demise
After withdrawing my hand
From games stacked against me.

.

CURSED

Witnessing love's infraction
Stained the template
Sealing the riddle
Cursing the heart
I buried deep in my chest,

Halting my desire
To drape a queen
Shadowing an angel's features
Weaving strands of my love
Between the seams
I'd squeeze together
Puckering the lips of textures
Created to kiss her softly forever

But I harbored a fear
That crafted my weaknesses
In front of perception
As she judged my foundation
By how easy it could be broken

Fearing,
I'd handle her
How they abandoned me,

Fearing
My need for her
Was way more than
She wanted me,

Visualizing success
Through philosophical stretches
Scratching theories
Into the inner layer

Of lenses
Not allowing me
To see what she really was.

.

SOUL SEARCH

Long stares
Set her sights on
Finding me
Within the darkness
Dilated rim of endless pits
Hallowed by the whistles
Echoing through the emptiness
Of black holes
Twisting the clouds
I used to be lost in
Around the pupil
Now blocking the sun
From shedding light on my pain

Love
Was the mistletoe dangling
Inside the threshold
Framing the gateway
Between heaven and hell
Swaying in the breeze
Of condensed whirlwinds
Defining my confliction

Sitting Indian style
In the middle of floors
Filling voids of lonely
With self love
But can't give
What you never had
Hyperextending my urge
To answer all her calls
Exposing my need of a hug

Loving the way
Her knowing how I felt
Held me together
Making nothing in this world
Able to take her from me

.

DEFIANCE

If actions speak louder than words
I wonder what symbols
Encrypt my body language
Onto the canvas of reality

But,
Can it really define me
If, what I am
Isn't what you see

If your process
Of cultivating impressions of me
Dissolving into the unraveling film
Tumbling off the roll
Into your equation of thought
As your eyes witness
My gestures sift
Through the judgement of pupils
To gain a perception

Will you find me worthy
Of the stories
Told by tears
Thinning the tissue

Layering a timid chest
No longer able to hide
Secrets between the lines

Of rib cages

Housing a mocking bird
Destined to sing love songs
To a heart
No longer able to feel itself beat

I wonder if eve
knew how detrimental
The taste of defeat
Could cringe the very nature
Of her purity
When her teeth
Broke the skin of that apple
Cursing woman
With that task of recreating life
To feel the pain
God felt after experiencing defiance

.

TREASURE CHESTED

Filthy hands
Cradled minerals
Materializing the darkness
Soiling the spoils of war,

Fingers would
Invade enemy lines
Scratching Earth's surface
Questing to pull a queen
Out of the mud,
But I often failed
Sacrificing nails
During scavenger hunts
Through uncharted territory

Clipping land mines
Shelling stones
Wedged between layers of defense
Fighting for position
Between the trenches
Those explosions left
Inside scarred tissue

Withering my hands
As they became
Vulnerable to infection

But if matches
Are made in heaven
Then long rubs in hell
Are already forgiven
Even though,
I still hoped
Her words could
Heal me through the pain
Of unconventional medicine,

I knew people
Would fail to understand the full picture
We planned to paint
Before feelings got mixed
And tainted the shades
That was supposed to let the light in

All those nights,
I used to just sit up
Watching your eyes chase dreams
Behind the curtains of eyelids
Right before she'd

Roll over and grab hold of me
As if she lost sight
Through the clouds of late night visions
Forcing her arm
To push open palms against timid sheets
Sailing fingers across ruffled waves of fabric
Until they reached me,

I became your lighthouse
To eliminate the things you felt
Hid in the dark
Since your pop was never around
Your perception of love was one sided

I used to feel like
My hands were too dirty
To clean off a diamond
Sifting through the rough
For so long
I became a mess
Over exposed to life's parasitic nature

I couldn't
See the holes in our boat
Through the flash
Of the sparkle in your eyes
Cherishing the result of my efforts
And not atoning for the sins
Of a buried treasure.

.

FLAG SHIP
My inner child,
Died as the captain
Of his relationship
With love

His life,
Flashed like lightning's fingers
Through the darkness
Of storm clouds
Squeezing thunder's wrath
Out of crumbled dreams

The flag ship he built
Wasn't strong enough to
Weather the storm of life
Anchoring his desire
To die with
What he refuses to lose hope in

So that
Wooden shell
Cased his heart
As he sunk
Deeper into my chest

Silly me
For convincing him that
A feeble mind could
Control a lucid dream

.

WARNING SHOT

I heard the shot,
Leave puckered lips
Stamping the message
Persuading breeze
Thrown in my face

Bowing my head
To check the status of my heart
As I close my eyes to listen
To how the sound of guilt
Froze moments in place
As shock clogs her joints
hearing her face tighten up

Before glancing over
At her mother's conviction
The power of spite
Frayed the strands
That intertwined us,
And
At that moment
I should of

severed the bond
And let time heal all wounds

Not knowing
That my ignorance
Would eventually cripple me

.

PROPHECY

I guess
Pontificating loves infidelity
Tainted my destiny
To remain
Wet behind the ears
Until fears of dry rotting
Unheard of and alone
Forced me to submit to
What was trying to settle me down,

If this
Birthmark on my tummy
Was my stamp of disapproval
The foreign parasite
Numbing one of my last
Instinctive sensations
Behind gut feelings

So my
So called love
Gets determined by brain fluids
After a open heart surgeon
Decides to handle your pain

And give you the joy you bring him,

But when her habits capitalize
On her deficiency with living a lie
He's forced to die twice

.

DEPRESSION

I too often die
Inside infatuated displacements
When my mind drifts
Like lost spaceships
Orbiting strange places
Becoming the deteriorating cocoon
Hiding a timid soul

I feel the oxygen
Escaping my happiness
As my aura seeps into the galaxy
Forcing my visions to fade
As they go astray
The gastric bypasses
That shine,
Like the stars they'll become
Through the darkness of me
Transcending further into my casket

Looking at
All the decisions I made
To get cornered off in this maze
But the freedom I chase

Deserves praise
I refuse to accept me
That's why I strive
To get the world to take note
Of how much I have changed

I hope I find my way
So my lost transmissions
Won't hunt for prey,

Cuz I too often get lost in space
In broad day
Sometimes reality itself
Forces me to run away
Sometimes I dream about
Dying while I'm awake
So I live in the heaven I created
so hell couldn't haunt me

.

SAVIOR

She was,
Who I needed to show up
My arms would reach past their limits
To gather every inch of her spirit
Fingers would spread
Until the webs felt
As if they could split
Reconstructing my palm
To feel more of her body
Allowing more of her
Wedging her feel
Between the gaps

It was worth elevating my thoughts
To shelter us in those dreams
I idolized,
The life I pushed for was worth
Those elaborate schemes
To have my words play
Vicariously through my actions

.

BRAIN WAVES

If I could just
Create brain waves
Able to arch my breaking point
Over these images
Stuck in my mind

I wonder if
That could rock the buoy
In the back of my throat
Forcing me to cough up
Exactly what I mean
On the canvas of my tongue
As taste buds sample colors
They'd gather
After it splashed
On its bristles

Regurgitating my urge
To convey emotion
On a visual platform
Illustrating hieroglyphics
Along the inner walls of my cheek
Defining the purpose of my words

As they take the shapes needed
To personify my illusions of art
So I'd speak vivid pictures
In the frame of a thousand words
As it rolls my points
Onto the empty canvas of my lips
Preparing to stamp the foundation
Of its audience

.

VICES OF LOVE

Watching how thoughts of you
Muster dream dust into motion
Cherishing the essence of you
Carrying memories
Into cloudy fixations
As I enter a daze

Replaying the movements
Of devils you danced with
And the ones
You live with too
You had no direction

Who gave you the right to judge me
All those nights with no lights
Winter breezes with no heat
Friday nights that became weekends
Fending for yourself
because mommy had young dreams
But some voids become landfills
When people don't realize
That they're filling it with garbage

Clinging onto the feeling of being distracted
House full of foreign aromas
You were burdened by situations
But I saw the power in your smile
And how you used to look at me
And how much I valued your time
I wanted to mean more to you
Because I already put you before myself

You struck life back into dreams
I killed way back when I was young
I wanted to grow old and die alone
But you made me feel
We could die as one
You made me feel
That sensation is the most valuable one
Your worth to me is the feeling of life itself

.

JUDGEMENT

Who were you to judge me?
See past the stale face.
Hiding the true me?

Who were you to tell me
My views were pessimistic?
Who were you
To define my way of thinking?

Back when it just became cool
For me to be myself?
Dress how I felt
As long as I didn't say too much
In fear I might scare the prey off
Attacking from the wrong angle
.

INNER VISIONS

Feeling like
Only I was destined
To see the vivid views
Dancing inside these dreams
My eyes
No longer show the way to my soul
Just blank stares
The milky layers of cataract
From cloudy trances
That shut out so much
People wondered if I was all there

But she saw the creator
She saw me scrambling to find myself
I needed you to tell me what I was thinking
I needed for them to confirm it
I needed to believe it
Fishing for confidence
I had none in me
You exposed how pathetic I was
I'm sure pieces of me still is
Off the strength of me being human

.

ATTRACTION

It was so hard for me to
Understand what love was
I'd get so attached to attraction
I felt the power of hope
Still reaching for someone reaching back
I couldn't feel anything holding me close.
I'd assume it was the pressures of life holding me back.

Pushing for that free feeling
And ended up free falling
Diving deeper into myself
I started to realize I'm the one that needed the most help
I needed to see happiness
I needed to witness love
So she told me she was pregnant

And I drowned in silence
Thinking how hard I'd have to grind
To raise myself

.

MUSTARD SEED

I wonder the nature
Of a seed
Able to soil itself

Are teary eyed dreams
Destined to sprout?
Or will they have to be nurtured ?
Watching how they
Placed him in a glass case
Shielding him from
Emotionally broken down faces
Crumbling over the lenses
He observed life through,

But I wondered
What kind of box

He'd create for himself,
Hovering my dark cloud
Over his incubation
Letting him witness
What the world made me
As my aura
Starts taking the shape of the room

Leaving nothing for light to consume
I felt my energy transcending
Through lines of sight I tried to
Fish my will through

Forcing him to fidget himself awake
For that brief moment
I swear I saw the shine of the sun
Light up from inside his face
As pink lips spread
Cracking a line through my cloud
Ruffling the wrinkles of joy into place
As his smile split the tension
Exposing his light to my shadow
As if to say it will be okay
I witnessed happiness

.

BLANK CANVAS

I watched a world
Get squeezed
Through an universal wormhole
That she entrusted to me,

Though I never noticed how
Vivid an empty canvas could be
In a room full of depictions
Trying to air dry wet paint
As life's brush
Strokes daily content onto us
As we grow closer to completion

Yet we all unconsciously
Handled this canvas
And managed not to
Rub off on it

I guess that's when it clicked

The big picture
Was the influences of us
How vibrantly we can
Share our energy

Despite the violent shades
Or rare disdainful tints
That's hard for us to face
But in turn still make us unique

To expose your whole self to the world
Is to kill the person you fear most.
And just like a Phoenix
Your soul will rise
From that feeling of hell
To recreate heaven in your mind
And the space your body occupies
Will feel heavens love.

.

PERCEPTION

Reality is a figment of perception
So it's only right for a man
To become everything he can't see
After a brain spins webs
Transparent enough
To string ideas along
The thin lines it knits
Between those sticky thorns
That dig into dreams
Struggling to get through to me
As I sleep,

Waking up during my funeral
Maybe it was
The lack of light in night air
Hindering my visions
But its time to face what I fear most,

I'm a product of thought
My light bulbs
Used to sit on a shelf

I never felt like
They got noticed
So I switched my method.
Writing the ingredients to the
Invested ideas

illuminating these shell casings
Which got some people to bite
But my life
Didn't practice what I preached

.

DISASTER

The scent of seawater
Tasted a little different this time
Love is a hurricane
But this one
Was filled with the spite
Of holy water
Baptizing karma in the irony
Of a hypocritical predator
Preying on the weaknesses
Reflecting off the mirror
He tried to break
Shattering a facade
Concealing the dagger
That pierced a main artery
While he pushes through the pile
Overexerting his weakened state
Until it immobilized his will to survive,

Forcing his fate to drown
Under the drum beat
Of emotional downpours
As he witnesses how
Rain drops bounce off the path
That lead him

To the end of his rope
Hanging in the balance
Of that four letter word
He couldn't put together
Before his visions faded
Into white canvases
After petty swipes of anger
Cleaned the slate

After all this time
I never noticed the pain
In your eyes
I never acknowledged
The light you provided
You were the sunshine
In the eye of the storm

I've been the captain
Of this relationship
For 6 years
Fighting to
Get through to you
Fighting to get away
From these troubled waters
Fighting to make sense

Of what kept us like this
But the day came
When I became
Too exhausted to fight
Laying on my back
Staring up at you in a new light

Feeling what every tear
Had to say about the stories
They came from
As your perceptions
Reincarnated feelings
That hit me as hard as they hit you
As each drop
Died on my face,

I was the man
All those other girls made me
But I was never man enough
To be myself around you
I never gave you my whole self
And blamed you for feeling empty
I never appreciated
The woman you were to me
I never told you

That you were beautiful
I never sacrificed my pride
I never surrendered my love
Held you when you cried
Explored what you held inside
Took her to do what you liked.

That need for true love
The very thing
I searched for my whole life

I guess
My faith wasn't strong enough
To carry my hope to its blessing

.

SELF

Weathering the storm
Made me a seasoned sailor
Laying stiff
Under the crust of dry salt
Healing the cuts
That scorn me

Drifting the Great Sea
As the clouds in my mind
Escape through cracked lips
Smiling through my sleep
Seems I finally died
So when I wake
Hopefully I'll be able to live in peace

No longer
Will women be my poison
Or society's opinions shape me
Time for me to focus on
Being the realist version of me
Becoming the man
My lady wants to be everything for
Finishing this book

So I can exist forever
Build my dream car
And go on long road trips
Enjoying the breeze
Show my kids
That it's okay to chase dreams
As long as you know
The key to achieving them
Is how far you're willing to reach

.

SOLITUDE

I've always been conscious
But this pain
Enlightened my darkness
I found myself
Through meditation

When she left
I sat alone for days
In a home we shared
Watching the span
Of our life flash before my eyes

As I died in the corner
Drowning in visions of us
Vanilla smiles
From the sweet Ole days
Lost in Manila skies

My first step
Crippled my idea of life
Under doubts weighing in on
Everything I began to question
Warping the platform
Of society's fabricated base
Designed to keep you safe
For as long as you stand on it

I chose to
Play the field
Carving my name in scars
Deep enough to
Scratch the surface
Of emotional hells within her

Burning inward
As she stomachs the thought
Of real love
Reverting back to a fictitious dream

She once gave up on
Before forgiving trust
To hand craft everything we built here
Filling the voided soul
Of a wholesome woman

But my fate
To plant my feet
On the freedom I desired most
Denounced the ways of the herd
While twisting the nature
Of the demons living within me

Watching her
Burn the recipe
That urged her gullible influence
With hope serving
Rotten food for thought
Upsetting the balance
Of her yen

As white clouds
Breastfeed raging fires
The milky remedy
To kill the high
Of peaking emotions
Forcing pieces of heaven
Within her
To sacrifice all their blessings
To cool the wrath of hell

.

MANIFESTATION

Natural disasters
Must run its course
Watching how tears
Fill the clouds in her eyes
Forecasting the approaching storm
Hacking lightning
Through the crashing sound of thunder
Fueling arguments as they escalate

Referencing history
From the index finger
We aimed our blame from

From where I sit now
I see the destructive nature
In that behavior
We only encourage confusion
When we attempt to define
Things that will eventually
Define itself

A repetitious lie
Becomes the truth
Or a perceptive opinion

Becomes a fact
After you build resumes
To shelter reference points
From how you saw situations
You scoped for proof
Missing the big picture
The reason most people
Have to be left alone before they see
How much of them is missing

Our defense mechanisms
Inflict the pain
We beg wisdom to prevent

So the more I felt
She wasn't for me
The more she saw the woman
She ain't have to be

I've been screaming freedom
This whole relationship
But when she gave me space
I'd rush to close the gap
I wanted the type of freedom
Society defined it as

When I really just needed
To be free enough to be myself

Feeling like her heart
Had no place for me
Made me feel convenient
So I pushed her away
To see how far she'd go for me

Labels were the propaganda
That justified my hatred
In the beliefs of a person
I never tried to understand
People that ride life's high
And numb the lows
Never achieve balance

I must accept the situations
God planned for me
I can't give in to weakness
I must let the universe align the stars
And arrange them in levels of importance
I must sit and let my pain heal my soul
If it doesn't burn it isn't working
If it wasn't meant

Then there's no need to ask for forgiveness
Matches were made in heaven
So long rubs in hell
Have already been forgiven

I'm just tired of running
Hiding inside distractions
To overcome something
I'll never face
Leaving that sore neglected
Increasing the chance of infection

.

QUEST

Footprints stamp leaves
With my impression of life
Turning over the pages
I conquered through time
As I pace through confined routes
On My quest for freedom

Thickening the skin
Layering the palm of steps
Opposing nature's obstruction
With misguided illusions
Lumping the boundaries
Of paths deeply rooted historians overstepped
While providing
The loose leafed pages
Wind swiped
From the grasp
Of branches stripping my darkness
Under the shadow of arms
Illustrating patterns
To confuse the direction
Of moon light

Prophesizing how
Light can hinder
Shades of grey areas
Undermining
The intuitive feel
Of soul searching

As I implanted my direction
On these pages
I engraved in the soil
Impressing the constellations
Peering through the clouds to see
How I documented my progress
Through the maze
I landmarked with my pain

Embedded in the stick and stone
That spike the sole of my feet
Mixing the minerals
Balancing the diet
Of rich soil
Giving up traditional beliefs
Down the unforgiving darkness
Of unpaved roads
Reconstructing the arches

Bridging my feet
To connect my destiny
With sacred passages
Harboring the hidden treasures
Deep inside pits of myself
If I ever become humble enough
To follow my heart into foreign lands

.

FAITH

Life's maze
Is riddled with pollution
The walls
Dim Faith's smile behind
Postages of propaganda's depiction

How deep is the space
That festers a lost mind
How many of us
Fall victim to lost transmissions

Sifting through the soot
Of sins created the texture of space
Blessings that came from that mud
Gave birth to the stars
We prey thankfully for
What they allowed us to achieve
Planets destinations
But our dying light
As the sun flickers
The demise of it all

And through
All these aspects of me
I cant even
Remember the sound
Of my true self
Speaking volumes
As I personified
His descriptions
Against the mirror
Puppeteering my motion
Through reality

But
I wasn't loyal
I stained his portrait
With flavors
Life seasoned me with
Justifying artificial evolution
With the compliments
That flooded my ego

Not taking heed
To his warning
Reaching out from pitched screams

Swinging off my earlobes
I, over shadowed dead weight
As he under minded
The foreshadowing of time's inverted humor
Grinning as he bared witness
To his fate knowing

I was destined to cry later
I stood at the podium
A false prophet
Cocky inside the features
Of the new me
But when i exposed my true colors
They flipped their love
And tried to erase me

Now
How steep is the ledge
I dangle from
Hanging onto woman
Begging for love
Clinging on to friends
Knowing ill always feel alone
Clenching dreams
Knowing my true desires don't exist
Grasping a hold of life

Not knowing what I have left to offer
Karma I paid for my sin
And all of its interest

I no longer believe
In my understanding of life
Became a student of experience
I no longer look for myself
In dark places
I've put my faith in urges
I only judge the feeling of vibes
My pain is self medicating
My redemption
Is the arch of my smile
Life is what I lived through
.

JOURNEY

Embarking on voyages
To self love
Taking my time
To watch my ways
Appointing the flaws
I'd like to change
Making myself
The first person I blame
You must show better
To see different..

Stop procrastinating
And build that woman
Infesting my dreams
Take her on long road trips
Show her off at car meets

Strengthening my soul
Through meditation
Waves of life
As I strive to master
Balance

Freeing my mind

From the pen
I caged these viewpoints from
To capture how life
Never ceases to amaze me

Maybe
Conquer my fear
Of the crowd I fell behind
After I take control of my life
Maybe I could lead the herd
From a platform
Overcoming my timid nature
Staring my biggest fear
In all of its eyes

And free myself
Through spoken word
Swirling wind with my tongue
Like how the hips of cursive
Bend letters out of shape
As I curve my lips
To show how
A heart can beat
Inside an old soul
Dying for you to love it

HIDDEN TALENT

Before this relationship set sail
I used to
Hide my emotions
Inside the ruffled covers
Of that notebook

A soulful kind of art
Like I illustrated it
With the jagged edge
Of my heart

But I wish
I could just speak
And let my soul seep
Through the cracks of my teeth
And just tell you
Just how much
Your love means to me
Without it sounding so cheap
But I can't

But you are
Becoming the cloud
I'm constantly stuck in
The heavy thought
That slouches me over
As I wonder
Was I ever really that special

But clouding my mind
With dark thoughts
Makes it so harder to see heaven

.

Thank you

For all your time =)